The Ten Rules of Reiki:

A Small Book with a Powerful Message

by Taggart King

www.reiki-evolution.co.uk

taggart@reiki-evolution.co.uk

Contents

About The 10 Rules of Reiki

Rediscover the Authentic Essence of Reiki

For over two decades, Reiki Master Teacher Taggart King has immersed himself in the profound wisdom of traditional Japanese Reiki. Now, he crystallizes his extensive experience of Reiki into ten transformative principles, taking you to the heart of this ancient spiritual and healing system.

"The Ten Rules of Reiki" is a guide that stresses the power of daily commitment to oneself, the significance of incorporating energy exercises and mindfulness into everyday routines, and the vital importance of self-treatment. But at its core, it champions simplicity and kindness towards oneself.

Reiki, in its truest form, isn't about striving for perfection or complicating the journey with endless thoughts and doubts. It's about approaching life and healing with a light heart, devoid of rigid expectations. Being content, keeping things simple, and maintaining a serene mental space are central to unlocking Reiki's potent energy.

Whether you're embarking on your Reiki journey or seeking to rejuvenate your existing practice, let these ten rules guide you towards a more profound, fulfilling connection with this timeless spiritual path.

(1) Reiki is all about you

Although in many circles, Reiki is seen as basically a hands-on healing system, a complementary therapy, something that you do to other people, it hasn't always been like that and if your Reiki is mainly about working on other people then you really are missing out on a system that has the potential to transform your life in so many ways!

If we go back to the origins of the system and Mikao Usui's original teachings, treating other people didn't feature a great deal at all: it was all about working on yourself.

We know that the word "Reiki" wasn't used by Usui, and that he referred to his system as a "method to achieve personal perfection", so that gives us a big hint as to the main thrust of his system: working on ourselves.

And I know that most Reiki systems will include hands-on self-treatments, and the precepts will be referred to, but there's a lot more to Usui's system in terms of self-healing, and spirituality, and self-development, if we can embrace the original practices and make them the foundation of what we do with Reiki.

What I'm talking about here are daily energy exercises and some form of self-treatment, I'm talking about the practice of mindfulness, and an ongoing focus on Mikao Usui's original precepts. When taken together, these practices when carried out on a regular basis have the potential to make such a difference to people.

Interestingly, I have heard some people saying that it's a bit selfish to use Reiki on yourself, that you should be spending your time working on other people, and I don't agree with this of course: it seems a very strange belief to choose.

Firstly, by treating other people you are also benefiting from the energy that you are channelling, so there's no way of separating out the energy so that it's only benefiting the person you're working on, and ignoring you.

Secondly, if we are following the Reiki system, following the precepts that deal with compassion and honesty, then how can we neglect ourselves? How can we deliberately refuse to nurture ourselves, refuse to give ourselves that special space in which to heal and balance?

I know it can be scary sometimes having to deal what's holding us back in our lives, and change can be frightening, but it's only by striving to be the best person that we can be – by letting go of emotions that are stifling us, by allowing the energy to heal us on all levels – that we can truly help others in the most powerful and positive way, because we can then channel the energy from a place of composure and mindfulness, a still calm vessel for the energy, channelled by someone who is a living embodiment of the many blessings that Reiki can bring into our lives.

So be an advert for what Reiki can do for you: work on yourself, let go of anger and worry, embrace compassion and forgiveness for yourself and embody the benefits of this wonderful system.

(2) Base your practice on the precepts

It's interesting that whereas in the Judaeo-Christian tradition we are given a list of things that we shouldn't do: "thou shalt not kill" etc, in Buddhism, followers are given a list of precepts or rules to live by that seem to be framed in more of a positive way.

And in Mikao Usui's system, he also provided his students with a simple, or apparently simple, set of precepts to follow, which seemed to be a way of distilling the essence of Tendai Buddhist principles into a form that anyone could understand. His five precepts have a long history, coming from a Tendai sect of Shugendo that Usui was in contact with, and this is what they are:

Just for today
Do not anger
Do not worry
Be humble
Be honest in your dealings with people
Be compassionate to yourself and others

The most important precept

For me, the first phrase is the most important, the "just for today...".

For me, this encapsulates all that follows it.

"Just for today" means being in a mindful state, fully engaged in the moment. If you are fully engaged with the present moment then you are in a state that is free from anger and worry, which are based on either dwelling on the past or imagining the future.

So "Just for today" means being in a state that is free from anger and free from worry. We don't want to distract ourselves through fear and we can remind ourselves that all is illusion.

We can simply exist in the moment.

And in that mindful space, you have the room to be compassionate, compassionate and forgiving towards other people and compassionate and forgiving towards yourself, being mindful means being in a centred, nurturing space where you can embrace honesty (and being honest with yourself is as important as being honest towards others) a space where you can truly experience the many blessings that you have in your life.

It all stems from, "Just for today".

The very heart of Usui's system

These five precepts are at the very heart of Usui's system and it was said that as much spiritual development could come through following the precepts as could come through carrying out the energy work.

So how can we work with the precepts?

Well we need to remind ourselves of them on a regular basis, and some people will say them out loud each day, perhaps as part of their routine of daily energy exercises and meditations. Maybe you could recite them in your head.

But it's not enough to just know what they are: the precepts need to infiltrate themselves into our daily lives, our thoughts, feelings and our behaviour. And we can achieve this in a couple of ways…

Firstly, we can ponder a particular precept, examining it and how it might have affected our lives, had we lived our lives by that precept in the past. How would we have behaved in past situations, how would we have reacted differently, or dealt with people, if we had embodied that particular precept?

1. What would we have felt, what would be have been thinking in different past situations if we were living that precept fully?
2. How would things have gone differently or been better for us and maybe for other people?
3. How would that precept have affected your relationships or your priorities?

Do some mental 're-runs' of past events and see how they would have been different had you been following that precept.

Doing this can provide you with some useful insights into how a particular precept can make your life flow more smoothly.

Precepts rehearsal

Secondly, what you can do is to imagine some future situations or scenarios, events where, based on what you have discovered about your past, you can imagine things going differently in the future.

Bring to mind typical future events or scenes which would benefit from the use of that precept, and imagine yourself in that future situation, embodying that precept, and notice how that future event runs its course; notice the differences in the way that you think and feel, become aware of the ways that you are behaving and reacting differently, responding to people differently.

Bring to mind clearly the new you who uses that precept as part of their daily life.

If you do this over a number of days, you will have a very clear idea of how the precepts could have changed past events in a positive way, and a solid understanding of how the precepts can be used by you in the future in different circumstances and events, how the precepts will work their way through your life, changing things for the better in many ways.

You can read more about "precepts rehearsal" in this blog post. Click the QR code below:

The precepts are something that we drip-feed into our daily lives, a work-in-progress where, over time, they become more and more a part of our basic blueprint.

We don't have to be perfect, though: we don't have to follow the precepts every waking moment and then beat ourselves up because we didn't achieve that. We are allowed to be human, we are allowed to not be perfect, which is all about embodying compassion and forgiveness for ourselves.

(3) Practise mindfulness

Although mindfulness is something that doesn't tend to turn up very often on most Reiki courses, it was actually a very important part of the system that Mikao was teaching, dovetailing with the precepts and the energy work to create a powerful method for self-healing and personal development.

And as you will have heard earlier, the practice of mindfulness is hidden in the Reiki precepts, hidden inside the phrase "just for today…" which for me is the most important part of the precepts: the phrase from which the other precepts flow.

So what is mindfulness?

Well mindfulness is a form of meditation that you can do anytime, anywhere.

You don't need to be sitting alone in a quiet room, setting aside time each day for your mindfulness practice: mindfulness is a meditation that can become part of your daily routines and activities. You can be mindful when you're doing the washing up, you can be mindful when you're eating your dinner, you can be mindful when you're typing on a keyboard or sipping cup of tea.

It is something that you can incorporate into your daily life as your daily life unfolds before you and it's not something that you need to set aside special time for, which makes it such a versatile way of meditating.

When you are mindful, you are consciously and fully aware of your thoughts and actions in the present moment, non-judgmentally, just existing in the moment, and in such a state you are free from thoughts of the past or the future, and free from the anger and the worry than can flow from such a dwelling on the past and the future.

By fully engaging with each moment, you are actually living your life, because all you have is this moment, this current awareness of the present: your life is a whole stream of present moments, and if you spend your time in the past and the future you are missing out on your life, because your life is here, now, not in the past, not in the future!

Find out more about mindfulness

The two books that I recommend about Mindfulness are both written by a Buddhist monk called Thich Nhat Hanh. The two books are "The Miracle of Mindfulness" and "Peace is every step: the path of mindfulness in everyday life".

I'd just like to read a small quote from Thich Nhat Hanh about mindfulness and washing dishes. Here goes:

"To my mind, the idea that doing dishes is unpleasant can occur only when you aren't doing them. Once you are standing in front of the sink with your sleeves rolled up and your hands in the warm water, it is really quite pleasant. I enjoy taking my time with each dish, being fully aware of the dish, the water, and each movement of my hands. I know that if I hurry in order to eat dessert sooner, the time of washing dishes will be unpleasant and not worth living. That would be a pity, for each minute, each second of life is a miracle. The dishes themselves and that fact that I am here washing them are miracles!"

So mindfulness is all about being fully aware of yourself, other people and your surroundings in the moment, focusing your awareness on each moment as it unfolds. And by doing that, you can savour each experience as it appears.

Getting started with Reiki mindfulness

Now obviously, when you start to practise mindfulness you are only going to gain little glimpses of that lovely 'in the moment' state, before your mind drags itself off to think about the past and the future, taking you away from your actual existence, and you need to be forgiving and compassionate.

This is a new way of doing things and it will take a while before your mind starts to understand how to do mindfulness consistently. Mindfulness is a work-in-progress and you'll find that over time those little glimpses of being 'in the moment' occur more frequently, you may find that occasionally you bliss out on some lovely mindful moments, and these moments, these glimpses, will build over time and become just a normal way of existing for you.

If your mind wanders, just gently bring your attention back to what you were doing, what you were experiencing.

There's no harm done.

Mindfulness lives in your Reiki practice already

You might be surprised to find that mindfulness is an integral part of your practice of Reiki.

When you're treating someone and you're in that lovely, merged state, blessed out on the energy, you're being mindful, just there in the moment, with the energy and the recipient, no expectations: that's mindfulness.

When you're sending distant healing, you've set your intent, maybe you've visualised something and you're just there, letting it happen, no thoughts of the past or future, just there with the energy: that's mindfulness.

So your mindfulness practice in your daily life – when doing the washing up, when eating a sandwich – will benefit your experience of mindfulness when using Reiki, and your experience of mindfulness when treating someone, or self-treating, or sending distant healing, will help you to experience mindfulness more easily during your everyday life.

You are training your mind, over time, to approach things in a different way, and your mind will learn what to do.

(4) Work on yourself daily

To get the most out of your Reiki, you need to have a regular practice of using the energy on yourself.

You're not going to gain the greatest benefits from this wonderful system that we all have if you just pick up Reiki once in a while, do something with it, and then put it down again for whatever period. So if you are looking for consistent benefits through Reiki then you need to have a consistent practice.

The precepts start by saying "just for today…" and we can extend that by saying, "Just for today I will do something with my Reiki".

And you can manage that; everyone can.

Everyone can make some time for Reiki each day because it doesn't have to be hours and hours and hours' worth. Do something for just 10 minutes: you have ten minutes. Do something for 20 minutes. And if you don't have 10 minutes then get up 10 minutes earlier in the morning: problem solved.

Everyone can find a way of doing something with their Reiki today, and we don't have to concern ourselves about tomorrow: tomorrow is another day. Tomorrow we'll start with "just for today I can do something with my Reiki", and we can find some time.

What could you do with your Reiki today?

Perhaps you're giving someone a full treatment, or perhaps you'll give someone a short blast of Reiki in your lunch-break: when you use Reiki on another person, you are gaining some benefit for yourself through channelling the energy. It doesn't pass through you without doing good things for you, and you'll be familiar with that lovely, chilled state that you experience as you get to the end of a Reiki session with someone else, almost as if you gain as much benefit as the person who's receiving!

Maybe someone has a bad back or a headache or an aching wrist: give them a short blast and snatch a little blissed-out-ness for yourself!

Can you take ten minutes in a lunch-break to become still and send some distant healing? That would be a lovely way to unwind and recharge your batteries half way through the day, while benefiting someone else at the same time.

Ten minutes of mindfulness and bathing in the energy at the same time.

Work on yourself in some way

You will have been taught a self-treatment method or methods, so use one on yourself, even if it's just for 10 minutes: you could just treat your shoulders, or rest your hands on your heart and solar plexus, which is a lovely way to experience the energy.

Have you tried that as a way of going off to sleep? The heat from your hands can be incredible sometimes, penetrating so deeply.

Take 10 minutes to do that for yourself, or maybe 15 minutes. Just drift with the energy as it flows. And of course you can do this for yourself whenever you're sitting down: do you sit at your desk reading something during your day: give yourself some Reiki as you do that.

Do you watch television? Reiki yourself as you do that and you might find that you start to drift off; that soap opera wasn't worth watching anyway! Preparing food... turn on your Reiki and channel it into what you're preparing: flood the kitchen with Reiki.

And you might be surprised how Reiki can turn itself on and flow when you're doing other things, particularly if you have some sort of a meditative practice that isn't Reiki: well, Reiki doesn't mind: it will turn itself on and click in, following your focus when you're doing any sort of meditation.

If you practise yoga or tai chi or chi kung:, Reiki will be there, being guided and moulded by your movements and visualisations, flowing and balancing and doing you good.

Build momentum

What's important here is the cumulative effect of using Reiki on yourself regularly, building momentum, small change building on previous small changes, taking you in the right direction for you.

Far better to do a bit each day than nothing for days and then doing a great big, long Reiki marathon on a weekend. That would be a wonderful experience, of course, and I'm not saying that you shouldn't do a mega Reiki session of you can, but make Reiki a regular part of your daily routine and you will be amazed by the benefits that this will bring you... remembering, of course, that you shouldn't beat yourself up if you don't manage to use Reiki every day.

Everything better than nothing is success and when we practise Reiki we embrace compassion and forgiveness, including forgiving ourselves for not being perfect, which of course we don't need to be in order to gain tremendous benefits from this simple spiritual system.

(5) Commitment is the key

There are spectacular benefits to be enjoyed through I've already spoken about the benefits that can come through the regular practise of Reiki, making working with the energy a regular part of your routine, trying to use the energy in some way each day.

The benefits of Reiki build up cumulatively, and sporadic and irregular practice won't be as effective in bringing you the very best that is possible for you through your Reiki.

Like many things, you'll get out of your Reiki what you are prepared to put into it, and Reiki deserves a little of your time each day. If you plug away, inch by inch, a few simple practices, a few simple routines, and make them a regular part of your daily and weekly routine, like brushing your teeth and brushing your hair – which you always make time for – then you'll get the very best out of your Reiki.

And once you have established your routine with Reiki it'll seem strange when you aren't doing your daily self-treatment or energy exercises, or distant healing. It doesn't take very long before your routine can just become part of who you are and it'll be difficult to avoid using your Reiki in some way.

So how do we commit to Reiki?

How do we make that decision, that final decision that cuts away all other possibilities?

Well I don't think you need to make such a decision. You just need to focus on today, and do something with your Reiki today, and that's all. And when the next day arrives, you repeat the process, doing something with your Reiki today.

One day at a time.

But there is something that you can do that can help you ease into your Reiki routine: visualise yourself doing what you intend to do.

Get yourself into a nice comfortable position and take a few deep breaths, perhaps do a bit of a self-treatment or part of hatsurei ho, to get the energy flowing, and imagine yourself doing what you plan to do: imagine yourself sitting down at lunchtime to do 10 minutes of distant healing, bring to mind how it will feel to send 15 minutes on a park bench just bringing the energy into your tanden and then flooding the energy out to the universe.

See yourself sitting on your sofa, blessed out for a while with an impromptu Reiki session, imagine yourself drifting off to sleep with your hands on your heart and solar plexus. See yourself doing these things as if you were watching yourself on a video, imagine how these things will feel, notice how you look and how your body seems so relaxed as you use your Reiki.

Imagine the benefits of doing this and see yourself experiencing those positive changes in the way that you behave and respond, those changes in the way that you feel about yourself and other people, changes in the way that you think. Just notice all those positive changes that come through your Reiki practice.

What you are doing here is mentally rehearsing what you days ahead, what your week ahead, will be like, and you are programming your mind to make these things happen, each day, to bring them to mind to remind you, to make them a priority.

Do this regularly and you'll be amazed by how simple it can be to ease into a really good routine with your Reiki.

(6) Don't try too hard

While we do need to commit ourselves and work with the energy regularly if we are to gain the greatest benefit through our connection to Reiki, working with mindfulness, focusing on the precepts and doing self treatments and other energy exercises as we can during our week, we also need to make sure that we aren't trying too hard at all this: it's supposed to be an enjoyable journey, not a big hard slog!

So we shouldn't take ourselves or our practice too seriously: Reiki is best enjoyed in a light-hearted fashion, in a gentle and laid-back way… not in a fists-clenched, furrowed-brow, tense 'read for a lot of hard work' sort of way.

We don't fore Reiki when we treat other people or when we work on ourselves and we shouldn't force a severe Reiki practice on ourselves either. That just wouldn't work: we should be doing our Reiki out of love, compassion, because we enjoy it.

Reiki is rather like a flowing stream and we're rather like a rough rock sitting in that stream.

The rock will become smooth over time but we can't force the river: the river flows at its own pace, it achieves its goals at its own speed and in its own way, and we accept the journey, allowing the water to flow consistently, doing what it needs to do to mould us into what we're becoming a tiny bit more each day.

There are several ways in which we can try too hard

Firstly, we might read about the experiences of other people when they do Reiki, when they self-treat, when they treat other people, when they receive attunements or empowerments. These people might experience particular things, see colours, have a particular sensation or a strong reaction and we might not be experiencing these things at the moment.

We think to ourselves, "I'm not doing it properly, I need to focus more, I need to do this better, I need to try harder to get it just right".

Well, no you don't.

We all have our own individual experiences when using Reiki. There are some people who see colours who wish they could feel tingling in their hands more. There are people whose hands fizz like crazy who wish they could see colours, and there are people who have very few sensations or experiences who wish they could experience something more than they currently are.

And things aren't set in stone, so what we experience now when using Reiki isn't representative of what we will notice as the energy flows. Things change, and we can develop our sensitivity to the energy through practice and through using special meditations that I have on my web site.

But what is not going to help is trying really hard, because Reiki works best, Reiki flows best when the person channelling the energy is chilled out and laid-back, just gently there with the energy, letting it happen, whatever is happening.

Just let it happen

Trying hard is a good way to put up barriers and slow your progress: they best way to progress with your Reiki is basically to give up and stop trying to do anything... just be there with the energy, no expectations, neutral, empty.

Just be, be mindful, notice what there is to notice, and if nothing's there to notice then notice that!

You will progress fastest when you stand aside metaphorically, do the exercises, just follow the instructions, be unconcerned by what you feel or don't feel, treat people, go through the motions, be unconcerned with what colours you might or might not see – it doesn't matter: be empty and compassionate and that's it.

Intuitive working

Another area where Reiki people might try too hard is when learning to work intuitively, and at Reiki Evolution we teach our students a method where they learn to allow their hands to drift with the energy to the right places to treat.

This approach works well for most people, though there are some whose intuition comes to them more in terms of images or words or an inner knowing, and that's fine too. But our basic approach is through hands drifting with the energy, rather like the hands being drawn like magnets to the right areas to treat, different from one person to another and from one session to another with the same person.

The key to success with our intuitive method is to not try: trying is actually the best way to stop it working, and the challenge that our students face is to learn to not do anything and not force anything, just to let it happen.

I remember a course that I ran in Cumbria several years ago where I was teaching this intuitive approach to Reiki practitioners and Masters. There were about 15-20 people on the course, we had treatment tables set up and there were perhaps 3-4 people to each table. One person was on the treatment couch and the others stood around the table practising allowing the energy to guide their hands. They all took turns on the table so everyone had the chance to practise on a few different people.

The method seemed to be working well for everyone except one poor woman whose hands were motionless, and remained motionless no matter how hard she tried to make the technique work. Of course it was her attempts to force it which were preventing her from achieving success with this method.

So what I did was to come and stand behind her and rest my hands on her shoulders.

Within a minute her hands started to drift. Now, this is not because I was giving her some sort of an 'energy boost' but because she was starting to have a bit of a Reiki treatment, and you know the feeling of melting and drifting and relaxing that this can bring, just within seconds. After a few moments she didn't care what was happening with her hands, she gave up trying, she drifted with the treatment – the merged with the energy – and her hands began to move to the right places to treat.

Having proved to herself that she could actually do this, she then went on to make the method work for her several times; she made it work by not trying to make it work, by giving up and not trying, by just being, in neutral, merged and empty.

And that's a good approach for Reiki work in general, I think.

You can read more about Reiki intuition in a series of four blog posts I wrote about this topic. Click the QR code below for Part I:

(7) You don't need to be perfect

Along with the need to be relaxed and laid-back and light-hearted about your Reiki practice, certainly not trying too hard, you should also make sure you're not beating yourself up for not being perfect.

Now, there is a precept that deals with this: just for today I will be compassionate towards myself and others, and that means forgiveness amongst other things: forgiveness for others and forgiveness for yourself.

Believing that you need to be perfect in everything that you do is an insidious belief and something that should not apply to your practice of Reiki. Just to make this completely clear: you do not need to be perfect to obtain benefits for yourself through Reiki, you do not need to be perfect when you're treating other people for them to receive all the benefits of Reiki.

Many different approaches work with Reiki, there is no exact way that things have to be done or carried out before they'll work, and Reiki is very accommodating.

But my mind wanders

Perhaps you mind wanders when you're treating someone.

So what?

This happens to everyone else and it'll happen to you. You will not mess up a Reiki treatment or be ineffective as a channel just because you were thinking about shopping for a while when you treated someone.

But how do you deal with a wandering mind?

Well, what you don't do is to try and force yourself to have an 'empty mind' – that will not work at all; that will make things worse because you now have two lots of thoughts: the original thoughts and all the new thoughts about getting rid of the first lot of thoughts!

Don't worry. Pay the thoughts no attention.

No need to focus on them. Just let them pass.

It doesn't matter, just bring your attention gently back to what you were doing, being mindful, merging with the energy and the recipient, letting it happen. And that's all you need to do, just be gentle with yourself.

Be light-hearted and compassionate

Will your mind wander again, having done that?

Probably, so just go through the procedure again: be light-hearted about it, be compassionate, let the thoughts go and bring your attention back to what you were doing.

Some treatments will probably be better than others in terms of a wandering mind, it'll sort itself out over time, and your mind will probably always wander some of the time. It doesn't matter. Do your best, make sure you're not forcing anything, and don't worry about it.

You're allowed to be human!

And there are other areas where you may well not do things perfectly, exactly according to the instructions, and it doesn't matter. If you're doing a self-treatment and you get the order of the hand positions wrong, it doesn't matter: Reiki will still flow, you'll still receive the benefit of the energy.

Maybe you realise that you forgot a stage that you usually carry out when treating someone: have you messed it up so they won't receive any benefit? No, Reiki will still have given them what they need.

Reiki is simple, Reiki works simply, Reiki rises above any set of rituals and rules that we might choose to follow, or forget to follow. You have a healing intent, and Reiki will follow that, and that is sufficient, no matter what you might say to yourself, or forget to say, or forget to do.

So don't worry.

Errors in Reiki attunements

Perhaps you're carrying out a Reiki attunement and you realise that you've missed out a section. Do you need to go back and do it all over again, apologising to the student for mis-attuning them?

No, it will still have worked fine.

There are so many different attunement styles in existence, with many different conflicting stages. Some attunements use a particular ritual that isn't present in other systems, other systems use stages that aren't present in your system. What is most important about attuning someone is your underlying intent, and the exact details of the ritual that you are using aren't so important.

By all means do your very best to carry out your attunement ritual according to the instructions that you were given, but also realise that there are no vital stages other than setting a definite intent when you begin; the rest is the icing on the cake, a set of movements, different in different lineages, that just help to remind you of what you want to happen, to support or focus your intent.

So you're fine.

You can be human.

(8) Don't keep trying to puzzle out 'why'

We've seen that the best state of mind to have when treating someone is to be empty and neutral, merged with the energy and merged with the recipient. We are in a mindful state, just being, not forcing things, letting it happen. If our mind wanders then we just gently bring our attention back to what we were doing, and bliss out on the energy.

And it would be nice if we could bring that lovely, centred, unconcerned state into other areas of our life, too, particularly when it comes to seeking answers or explanations for everything that is happening to us and to the people that we are treating.

Because if we seek answers or explanations for every little sensation that we have, every little happening, and particularly if we can't be content with a practice or an approach without understanding exactly why we are doing a particular thing, then we are going to make our journey with Reiki a particularly difficult one.

What do colours mean?

If you see a particular colour, or colours, when treating someone, or when self-treating, it might be nice just to accept this as a pretty light-show, an added bonus, a colourful and welcome side-effect of the flow of energy… rather than trying to puzzle out why you had a particular colour and what that means.

Maybe the colour does have a meaning – there are colours associated with the chakras for example – and maybe the energy was focusing on a particular chakra when you saw that colour. But because Reiki works on so many levels, because it deals with physical things, mental states, emotions, spiritual aspects, because it deals with historical problems that are still present in some way in our energy body, and it deals with things that are 'on the boil' and haven't manifested yet... we have no real idea of what it's doing other than to be safe in the knowledge that the energy is giving us or the recipient what we need.

So stop trying to puzzle things out: it will make no difference to your experience of the energy or the effectiveness of your Reiki.

Get your head out of the equation and just let the energy do what it needs to do, without all that frantic mental activity!

What do sensations mean?

If you have a particular sensation when treating someone, or you were drawn to a particular area of the body, do you really need to know why that happened?

If your hands ends up resting on someone's liver area, does that mean they have liver disease?

No, it doesn't, it just means that the energy needs to flow there to produce the balance that is appropriate for the recipient.

We don't diagnose with Reiki: Doctors diagnose. Reiki Practitioners and Reiki Masters don't diagnose, and shouldn't diagnose, and if they feel an urge to diagnose something then they should stop it.

In any case, Reiki works on lots of levels, so in Traditional Chinese Medicine the liver is said to hold mental states and emotions that might be being dealt with; is that what's happening? Who knows? We don't need to know, we can just accept that Reiki is doing what it needs to do, and go with the flow, merging with the energy in a lovely mindful state.

Let's speculate!

Worse still is the urge to try and come up with our own theories about what we are feeling.

Some people start to think in terms of blockages or negative energy or, worse still, 'dark energy'. Those are not helpful terms to use when talking to a Reiki client, who came in looking forward to a lovely blissful session and come out with a belief that they are harbouring a blockage or dark energy.

We don't need to introduce such ideas into our Reiki because they're not helpful to us or the people that we work on.

The sooner we can accept that Reiki is all a bit mysterious and puzzling, but works tremendously well, so we can just let it do what it needs to do without second guessing what's happening, the better it will be for us because we can just let go of all those questions and enjoy the journey.

Did I really feel that?

Actually, along with thinking too much and questioning everything comes the challenge that we can face when second-guessing things that we feel or notice.

Did I really feel that sensation, was I making it up, is it all in my head, did I only feel something because I wanted to?

Well, either you feel something or you don't. If you feel something you can trust that you felt it; you can't make yourself feel something. If it was possible to fool yourself into feeling Reiki sensations then everyone would feel something and there would be no-one who was concerned that they don't feel anything when doing Reiki… they would all have magicked sensations into existence, wouldn't they?

So just accept and go with what you feel: if you notice a lot of energy flowing into a part of someone's body (maybe your hands are fizzing or tingling or pulsing or whatever sensation you have) then just stay there for longer until you feel the flow of energy subside.

You can trust what you're feeling.

You're not making it up.

(9) Trust your intuition

Along with doubts about whether people are fooling themselves when they notice the flow of energy, come doubts about a person's intuitive ability.

Am I really feeling drawn to that part of the body or am I fooling myself? I heard a word or phrase in my head, or I saw an image, is this all in my head? Am I making it up?

Did my hand really feel like it was being pulled like a magnet to the person's knee, or is this only because I know that they had an injury there?

You need to know something: you are intuitive. Everyone is intuitive.

You may not be used to noticing the intuitive messages that your body and mind are sending you, but they have always been there.

Are you making it up? Yes, in a way: nobody else is giving you this information, it's coming from you, from that intuitive part of you that generates such messages and insights, or that 'inner knowing'.

Intuition can come to you in different ways

Maybe when treating someone you feel strangely drawn to a particular area of their body, your attention wants to rest there or dwell there. It might not make any sense, but that doesn't matter.

Just go with what's coming to you and direct the energy there, resting your hands or hovering your hands over that area.

Maybe when you're self-treating, you feel drawn to a particular area of your body, well just focus your attention there and allow the energy to flow there.

Just accept what comes to you and work with it.

Some people have intuition come to them in terms of visual images or words or muscle movements: everyone's different. Don't assume that this isn't real intuition, that because it's you and you're not intuitive, this can only be just nonsense.

Just stop thinking and stop worrying and stop second-guessing yourself, and cultivate the lovely mindful state that you enjoy when giving Reiki.

Ease into that lovely merged state and just accept what's coming to you, allowing the energy to guide you in its own way, because you are already as intuitive as you need to be, and the way to access your intuition is to just merge with the energy, and let it happen.

(10) Ignore silly rules and restrictions

Another problem with thinking too much is that we can start to overcomplicate something that is a very simple and a very safe way of helping ourselves and helping other people to change things for the better. And if we think too much, and particularly if we start to worry too much – and I have to say that there is something in the Reiki precepts about worry – we end up with people speculating about potential dangers, imaginary dangers, problems that have no basis in anyone's experience, and we start to limit our practice of Reiki.

And you can see that in different lineages, where students are taught long lists of situations where they shouldn't use Reiki, people that they shouldn't treat, things that they have to do, or should always do, or should never do, and many of these restrictions and limitations are just complete nonsense, completely divorced from reality.

And students take these teaching on in good faith, and pass them on to their students when they become teachers, never questioning whether what they were taught has any basis in fact or experience.

Reiki contraindications

So what restrictions do we have careering around the world of Reiki? Take a look at these examples:

- You shouldn't treat people who are wearing contact lenses
- You shouldn't treat people who have cancer
- You shouldn't treat babies
- You shouldn't treat people who have a broken bone
- You shouldn't treat pregnant women

- You shouldn't treat people with high blood pressure
- You shouldn't treat people who have pacemakers
- You shouldn't treat diabetics
- You shouldn't treat people who are stressed.

These are nonsense and have no basis because Reiki is a safe and nurturing energy that gives people what they need.

So, where is the evidence that using Reiki makes people's pacemakers explode? Where is the research paper that proves this? Or even if there isn't a research paper, where are the anecdotes, where it is clear that Reiki messed up a pacemaker?

Where is the evidence? There is none.

Where is the evidence that you shouldn't treat people who are stressed? There is none.

Good grief this is nonsense isn't it?

Some people are taught that you shouldn't treat clients with cancer because the Reiki will 'feed the cancer'. OK, where's the evidence? And also, since everyone listening to this track has some cancer cells in their body, cells that have gone wrong and which are mopped up routinely by our immune system, we shouldn't be treating anyone, including ourselves!

It would be a death sentence.

Some people are taught that they shouldn't treat pregnant women. OK, where's the evidence that Reiki is dangerous? There is none, of course. But because sometimes women can be pregnant without knowing it yet, particularly in the early stages, if you believe that Reiki is dangerous to pregnant women then you should be refusing to treat any woman of childbearing age just to make sure that you're not treating someone who might be pregnant.

And if you're attuned to Reiki yourself, then of course you would need to make sure that you never had children.

It's all about worrying too much

What all these rules and restrictions do is to introduce into Reiki something that Reiki is designed to ease: worry, worry about what's going to happen, restricting what we do 'just to be on the safe side', all based on wild and feverish imaginings that are passed on from teacher to student.

Well, Reiki is bigger than that and need not be restricted.

And another area where Reiki does not need to be restricted is in terms of what we are told that we have to do in order to work with Reiki.

There are Reiki people out there who have been taught a fifteen-stage process or ritual that they need to go through before they start a Reiki treatment. If they don't get it right, well they've been told that it isn't going to work properly and so they worry about that, as you would, but of course such rituals are optional: you don't have to go through a 15-stage process before you give someone a Reiki treatment.

Someone somewhere made up the ritual and then it's ended up being passed on to people as gospel, as dogma.

There are some Reiki people out there who have been taught that they have to draw the Reiki symbols on their palms every day because if they don't then the symbols won't work for them. People are told that you have to draw the three Reiki symbols over your palms before you give someone a treatment, or that you have to draw the three symbols over every hand position that you use.

Reiki is very simple, you know

You plonk your hands on someone, shut your eyes if you like, and the energy flows.

Much more than that is really gilding the lily.

And I know that some rituals can be useful: they help you to focus your attention, they help you to focus your intent in a particular way, and some people like rituals and there's nothing wrong with that.

But we should remember that Reiki is a very simple system, it works brilliantly without clutter, and if we use processes and visualisations and set phrases, we should remember that these are actually optional, not compulsory.

We can experiment and find our own comfortable way with the energy, different from the way that other people work, and that's fine.

The Ten Rules of Reiki in a few sentences

If I was going to try and sum up the ten rules of Reiki in just a few sentences, I would say this:

To get the most out of your Reiki, I recommend that you make a commitment to yourself to work on yourself daily in some way as your top priority, but not beating yourself up if you miss the occasional day.

Use energy exercises, self-treat, focus on the precepts regularly and drip-feed mindfulness into your daily activities and routines.

Don't try too hard, though: be light-hearted and forgiving towards yourself because you don't have to be perfect.

Try not to clutter your mind with lots of thoughts and doubts and questions: just be neutral, have no expectations, be empty and content.

And make sure you keep things simple. Reiki works best when it's simple.

About the Author

Taggart King is a Reiki Master Teacher, Cognitive Hypnotherapist and NLP Master Practitioner who has been teaching Japanese-style Reiki through live and then home study courses for over 20 years.

He founded Reiki Evolution in 1998.

Taggart has written eight books about Reiki, created several Reiki-related journals and recorded a dozen audio collections (on CD and MP3) comprising guided meditations and audio commentary to accompany all the Reiki levels and practices.

Reiki Evolution

Reiki Evolution offers small-scale Reiki courses through a team of 'trusted teachers' in the UK, all of whom offer Taggart's style of Reiki courses. There are never more than 4-6 students on any course so we can give you individual attention.

And finally, Taggart teaches Reiki mainly through home study courses.

Cognitive Hypnotherapy

Taggart qualified as a Cognitive Hypnotherapist in 2010, and as a NLP Master Practitioner, with The Quest Institute, training with its founder, Trevor Silvester.

He has also assisted in the training of new students on the Quest Diploma and NLP Master Practitioner courses.

Printed in Great Britain
by Amazon

28488272R00026